Bring Me Into Flesh

by

Rosie Rosenzweig

Ibbetson Street Press
25 School Street
Somerville MA 02143

www.ibbetsonpress.com

ISBN 978-0-359-99338-3

Cover art by Joy Langer
Joy Langer, a New York Yoga instructor, is an artist whose specialty has
been domestic murals. For more information go to: www.joylanger.com

Book design by S.R. Glines
text: Adobe Garamond Pro

Acknowledgements

Earlier versions of some of these poems have been published in the
*Jewish Women's Literary Annual, Journal for the Association of Research
in Mothering, The Mom Egg, Neshama Magazine*, and *Lichora*. "The
Western Wall" and "Let Me Not Be Afraid" appeared in her book *The
Jewish Mother in Shangri-la* (Shambhala Publications). Earlier Versions
of "I Miss the Dreams," "Caught in a Cave," "Let Me Not Be Afraid,"
"The Pleading Time," "The High Holy Day," "Heaven Must Be a Stand
of Lilies," "I Feed the Image of a Sister," "Before the Crossing," and "As
long as comfort lives" appeared in Congregation Beth El's various original
prayer books called *Vetaher Libenu* (Open our Hearts), *Rofenu* (Heal Us),
Hazicharat Nishmot (The Memory of Souls) (Sudbury MA). "The Buddha
with A Tallis " sequence was part of an exhibit at Brandeis University's
Women's Studies Research Center with Linda J. Hirsch's photograph.
Another version of "Before the Crossing" was set to music by composer
Beth Denisch and performed at a Berklee College of Music concert in
November 2007.

Contents

Part One

Part Two

Part Three

Part Four

Part One

Bring Me into Flesh

"Frum Europe is gekumin my cousine,
Shein ve gold un lichtik ve a greene
Bekelach is roite ve pomegrantzen
Und fiselach vos betten noch to tanzten."
De Greene Cousine.

Skipping ahead of her friends,
hair riding on its own breeze,
a cheerful face gracing a Victorian dress,
she glided into my sights.

Was this a prophecy, or just my need?
I knew her, a leader among them,
before she knew me. Performing
on the pressed-dirt path,

she imagined it a dance floor,
sparkled her eyes, brought color to her cheek,
and blossomed into blush. A green sprout,
soon a flower to bloom, she was loved.

I watched her as she was courted, possessed,
then, catching her breath, taken to bride.
And I waited for him to drop his seed
and bring me into flesh.

Hush! The baby is awake!

"Shah! Ze shloft nit!"
Newly turned from the other world,
I moved my eyes towards the voice.

Through the striped wooden slats,
I saw them unfold themselves
from one another, and stare at me.

My arms and legs waved themselves,
as I tried to turn and look.
I felt my sheets turn wet
and a white ceiling lowered to meet me.

My mother, brimming with milk,
caught my ribs, raised and
rocked me with a Yiddish lullaby.
I gagged as she leaked on the rug.

Communal Bathroom

Sitting on the sink, my new potty,
because the main plumbing was occupied,
I watched my mother teach the fine points of toiletry.

Washing the hands and the face
I imitated mom's boobling sounds and sighs.
It was supposed to be fun.

Without diapers, I now qualified
for a baby-sitter: my mother's Yiddish landsman,
the old world countryman. Moshe with the drooping lids,

eyes hidden by hooded flesh,
enlivened a young girl's innocence.
and initiated her ongoing quest for words.

I became a chatty girl giving away childhood secrets,
guarded by a new nanny during parental outings:
the back seat crib of my uncle's car.

The Haskalah*

My father, a Polish cantor, a peddler,
went along busheling out his songs,
up and down Canadian streets:
— *Two pound potatoes for ah quarteh!*

The wives would come all haggling for their price.
After his run, the horse and buggy pranced back
   to our back yard stall,

Or so I dream those years before my birth.
The horse burned in a barnyard fire,
his rider played out his deck:
   black ace lying by his queen
   with spadefuls for his grave.

His Yiddish exile-lullabies play
tangos from Thieresenstadt;
children singing alphabets by a lonely stove;
my own hushed humming at my mother's end:
   Rosinkes mitt mandlen —
   Raisins and cupcakes your father will bring,
   And when you arrive the angels will sing. . .

* The Haskalah (a movement that motivated thousands of emigrants to leave
  Europe for America) is the Yiddish word for the Jewish Enlightenment, a
  secular rebellion against Orthodox Judaism.

A High Priest's Daughter: the Kohenit

They forgot to engrave the hands,
forked like the Doctor Spock's Vulcan oath,
into his tombstone.

Standing on the prayer bench
to kiss his cheek, I remember his left arm
round my neck in the men's section.

On the rabbi's signal, he sent me back to my mother
hidden behind the women's veiled balcony,
as he ascended to the lectern and raised

his prayer shawl over his face.
Holding his forked hands high to bless us
with the mudra of a *Kohen*
(pinkie and ring finger touching,

forefinger and middle together)
he sang quietly in his perfect tenor.

As he intoned the Divine attributes,
we all pleaded and prayed
to ban our monstrous dreams from our sleep.

Hostage to Fortune

Sometimes the acorn drops
close to the trees,
sometimes, depending on the wind-stop,
its seizes nothing.

Sometimes it rides hobo-style
in the guts of wings,
and relieving itself, tumbles headlong
open-mouthed to catch the earth.

It can part and tag the ground with strong young roots.
unsheathing a greedy toss of leafy flags.
It claims dominance over all it sees.

Scorning the growth that birthed it,
the seed, like me, rises slowly,
like a stranger from a strange land.

Migration: After Moshe

I dreamt of far flung flights,
singing to the God-watched sparrows.
I believed then in the watch.

I called to the blackbirds, the grackles,
even the ones with the red chips
on their shoulders: *Hey, don't you know me?*

I became an eagle, flying in from Nova Scotia,
covering the leagues with one wing flap, and
floating to the highest seaside crags.

I held the air still, and dived with needle sharp aim.

Grooming my new jungle-plover feathers
with my beak, my hunger emboldened me
to pick the teeth of crocodiles.

I incarnated the original Bird of Paradise, and
with a wing span towering over the curving earth,
cradled it in my fine-haired palm.

After the Letter Came

After the letter came about the 83,
(or was it 87? My mother could
never remember)
she forgot how to be happy.

She sat at her window,
wringing and caressing
her palms over her knuckles,
with her tears over her sobs.

This were her refrain:
Geharget and geshtorben, murdered and dead;
it was my bedtime prayers, my morning song
my after-meal blessing, holding my face in her hands.

With no more letters from her parents,
her sisters, her brothers, her aunts, uncles, cousins,
this *greene cousine* with cheeks red like pomgranets,
whose feet desired once to dance,
danced less and less,
laughed less than more,
and continued to croon:
Geharget and geshtorben, murdered and dead,
holding her face in her hands.

So she hugged us more,
my big brother, my big sister,
and me, always the baby, and she cooked more,
and she cleaned more, and much more,
she said I love you, I love you, much, much more,
with their photos, and their letters
and their faces in her hands,
in a country where the streets
were not paved with gold,

and where no one held her face in their hands.

Reprieve from Study

The hard lily of their formation floated
wisps across the sun. There was a hundred,
at least a hundred of them, each with one
white stripe thrown back lightly

along the wind. Their awkward grace
styled itself through those long
necks, then moved slowly into large wide
wings. They were still

against a moving sky: I
was fastened by their common
arrowhead. In a moment,
they set down flat-footed

on the field, and waddled
with their gaggle knobby-wise.
Then I undid myself from my desk to follow
the fresh smell they pushed down from the north.

I creaked by rose-hid gates, and sneaked
beyond the back garden; when I
combed by, I bent the long-stemmed field.
A tight breath slimmed my chest as I warped

through the marsh grass wrinkling
the land with my belly; my spine
pulled at the whole length of me, gathered
me together, and pushed me on ahead.

I even reached
to touch them, while above me
a black crow circled. I felt my skin grow
scales; my tongue held tight. No help. He cawed

his find to the sky. Their thunder
struck me just ten yards short with my loss caught,
heavy and round, like an apple in my throat.

Rites of Re-enactment: Patriot's Day 1976

"O! Ye that love mankind ...
Freedom hath been hunted around the globe ... "
<u>Common Sense</u> *by Thomas Paine*

Concord has mown the battle green,
straightened the boards on the Old North Bridge,
and arranged for parking. Vendors
have set up their one-day stands
for plastic horns. Canoes gather
close by the bridge to see first shots fired again.

Some son of the American Revolution,
his white wig freshly cleaned,
begins to march his redcoats down Main Street.
The patriots are down by the river.

Each town with matching uniforms carries its own standard.
One, for authenticity even dressed in motley.
A camera, thinning them into celluloid,
catches the play in its moving coil.

A long pause holds the air still:
the known words about the whites of their eyes emote,
and cap-gun powder sprays the actors.

You are there, caught in the crossfire!
A child, hoping for intermission, covers his eyes with his collar.
After the theatricals persist, the rifling stops;
a prisoner is taken, snakes his red arms around his gun, and
waves to the prompters on the sidelines;
plastic horns whine through the pine trees.

Uproad, the Minuteman statue fixes his sights beyond the craning tourists.
One lone veteran wrinkled and damp from the rain,
waves his peace banner dissenting quietly on historic ground.
Marching around the flagpole on the Lexington Village Green,
we offer Sunday rites for the liberty tree.

The Boy I Didn't Marry

Sitting with the boy
I did not marry, or even date,
I caught one brief thrill at the high school reunion.
I was 17 with a throbbing groin wishing for *le mot just*.

He was such a gorgeous *goy*, an honor student,
who morphed the bad boys into the jazz band,
who probably by then had strummed his way
into women up and down the east and west coast,
singing over the contours of their bodies
thrusting his lyric poems with the extra large words.

I can barely remember his shrewd slanted smile.
Whispering imagination into my ears,
he had no cavities, and no distinctive smell.
Without restriction from a protective broken-English mama,
he embodied the aristocracy of the pure Canadian,
full of fresh air from Hudson Bay stock.

Tortured by convention and conscience,
structured into the wannabe writer role,
struggling through incompetent suicidal dramas,
I traveled far to find this exact and skillful experience.

In parallel play, I blushed and danced away.
All I have now is this forensic vapor of memory,
a scene that may have never happened.

All I really have now are these words.

Part Two

A Wash of Waves
For Schulem

a wash of waves
and each wave
remembers others
who remember me.

A roll of facts
photographs the mood.
but none moves me
save you

who walks beside this seascape,
not just arms and legs,
but body, breath and sound
singing to the sea
in me.

The Western Wall

The rocks are bursting in this, the place of rocks,
stones standing on the shoulders of other stones,
a wall whose words rise up from the sealed bonds of memory.

Hymns sound, spread, and fly
like the preened wings of birds
who court and search the landscape for their place,
a nest within the shrubs, bursting with bush above our heads.
These roots hold the heart of the wall.

Boulders, like ancient stairs, raise a stairway,
each rise a note, each step a new prayer,
with praise and pleas that multiply and wail
like a chorus of blues-singers
skit-skatting up the scale from their bottom-base,
from their pit of this old-time ruin.

They tell of temple-times and by those tales,
climb up beyond the peaks of turrets.
The wall grows bright and brighter at each round.
Daughter to these prayers, can I join this reach
and blend with the sun and moon and stars and clouds?

I want to be the wall, homeland for these birds,
who roost, flutter and hover here in this sweet peak of light.
Yearning to become one mouth with You,
I crave to sing in choir, note by note, to rebuild rock by pillar,
And to become myself with You.

Malignant

I

You said the word,
once whispered by the generation before;
you said the word again
out loud with a hurried resignation,
the way the doctor must have decreed.

A mortal hush held my chest tight;
Without movement, I sat watching your lips close.

I wished a fence, a wall, a prayer
would gather, build, circle and protect us
with the promise of never-ending life.

II

Catastrophe chastens me:
your thought becomes a wish becomes a deed -
is it enough? Will there be time to bring these little gifts?

A day dream of green, not even a request,
and I have grown a garden for your one moment's pleasing bloom;
to maintain calm, time must only be in the present tense.

I will buy the pillow for your porch chaise;
I will plant the lilacs within your view;
find the most comfortable chair, the choicest cut, and
any book you want to quiet the nag of convalescence.

III

Waiting for treatment, seconds stretch to years:
white- coated messengers test, analyze, and report the news.
No secrets here. Sages say this life is a waiting room for the next.

But which door leads to where and why?

IV

I have to choose: the princess or the tiger,
or so says the fable with thresholds to tomorrow.

Is the wild beast really our fateful end?
Or is it a mystic light in disguise?

V

I would comfort you with the full-headed scent of flowers
not cut flowers, abandoned bodies, thirsty for a full vase of water.

I will nurture flowers with their full roots gripping
and feeding the luxury of life, -

flowers blooming, rising, praising their time to live
and their time to seed, - a seed to redeem your future life.

I Fed the Image of a Sister

I fed the image of a sister
bloated by despair, burdened by her heartbeats,
warmed double by the anger round her neck.
Jostled and strung taut by her going,
I looked for her in all the women that I met.

I nurtured a rack of bones, my brother
sacked and sewn after a cutting,
bagged into a bed too soon to know himself,
his young dreams blown over the hills of clouds.
I looked for him in every man I knew.

I held my father, oh my father,
laid out in a velvet paper box,
lowered with a faltering crank,
covered with my handfuls of dark soil.
I grow a memory of him that is not him.

Someone else can look for fathers,
hear them out in old age homes,
silent men who allow me silence,
while with my mother, I listened
for the seeding of my own green time.

Bermuda: She Can Still Hear the Crickets

She can still hear the crickets shrilling and
rubbing their wings through the night till dawn.
Her ceiling light blackened a hole into the next day.

Innocent as how a broken heart can seduce,
she wept in the dining room at her lover's quarrel.
Holding his glass of wine, the Social Director forced the lock to enter.

He tied her hands while she called him Moshe,
as if she were still a little girl being punished
and puzzled by this beating in the groin.

The Best China

taking
the dish
from the bottom
the very bottom shelf
the most worn
the oldest one
the one with the largest chip
on the the rim
discovering the joy of a pinprick
caressing the break
fingering again the chipped edge
enjoying the sharpness of it,
pleasuring the cut on the finger
the letting go of my blood
knowing that the best china is safe
on the top
the uppermost shelf
its secret
beyond reach

For a Glimpse of You

"I will put you in a cleft of the rock. ..."
Exodus 33:22-23

I have lingered in the cleft of rocks
clinging like a bird to the lip of a cave,
my broken words ruined about me like rubble.

I have longed for more than my mortality
and battered at eternal gates
for more than my own will.

You answered with the spoils
of flowers before their seed was ripe.
Still I pleaded and pursued:

I needed you as evening needs the stars.
I wanted you full face again to me.
In answer, your afterthought of presence

burned the shadows into a lonely earth.
I felt you near, but dared not look, and
I heard the sweet silence of your breath.

Finally, you redeemed me with a soundless rustle
brushing through my welcoming limbs.
When you left, your absence spoke to me
where no words would be heard.

Don't Touch the Grass

Don't touch the grass with bare feet.
It will seduce you.
Pull your legs into a soft controlled stroll
with your toes curled. If you open them,
soft slithery blades will crevice and caress their crotch;
You cannot resist. Beware.

I have built a makeshift lattice fence
to guard the children. Even though they love life,
I will *not* be influenced. I talk to myself
as I thoughtlessly make rainbows with my hose,
and water the desperately parched new trees.

I even withhold my smile from the young rabbits flirting, teasing,
and hopping over each other before they turn
to face their young love again.

I scold myself: *"Turn, run and enter the house immediately!"*
My poems have become invisible, rotting
like compost feeding the roots of plants and trees.

The Sign Says: "Men Working"

Running on empty, I am commanded to stop
between frantically scheduled errands.
Reluctantly, I pause. my car.

Blinded by the hoo-haw of flashing lights,
my hybrid is shadowed by a hovering ladder,
flaplessly, like a hawk eyeing a miniscule snack.
Two white trucks, brimming
with metal hats and men, are the audience.

The yellow jacket in the cage above
leers at my cutoffs, my shell bra camisole
fresh from the gym's boutique.
My sheer over shirt hides my wrinkles.

With an unseen string,
the sheriff pulls me past the parade.
The blue collar under the fuchsia police cap
slings his large wrench like a master's baton.

Every home I pass holds invisible workers
tending children, teaching them
to picket with neon signs:
"Women *always* at work!"

Like a Lover

Death, court me like a lover in my dreams,
keep me sweet with grief,
and safe with anger and its cause.
I need a bold beginning after a pause.

Quietly, with a brief slight of hand,
hold me secret from my family's eyes.
It is harder to meet their fire in the noonbright,
than covet your sly glance by shadowlight.

A still small turn to dawn could wake belief
if I could wait. If, by and by, I remember
the sweet elusive warmth of early love.
this affair could pass,

and leave me whole.
I wished for the slow wet yes touching growth,
 importance in the smallest things,
and a quick sealed passage out of life.

I Watched My Daughter Dive

"… the poem framed in lines, an aphorism of experience."

I watched my daughter dive,
the moving light moved by her body;
she was a flow in the circle of a lifeline.

It was so hard to watch.
to be
just there,
to not reach out,
to not slice,
one linear movement in a frame,
and to allow the dance on the board,
and the leap,
the fresh plunge,
o
from that long time under water,
to the bubble up
to find a new breath
and float

For a Broken Wrist

For my wrist surgeon, Dr. Phil Blasar

Let us now praise the wonder of the hand,
lunch for a rabid fox near my mailbox.
My sinews are so intricate, my bones so numerous,
my fingers so cunning, wagging like coyotes' tails.

I can move my pinkie now, but the wrist carps back.
I make a fist and a den of sly bones slide
in electric co-ordination like a silent symphony.
I can hear that in my elbow.

I have forgotten how to pray;
I must have forgotten Jerusalem,
to invite damage to this small span of limbs,
to make my right hand lose its cunning, and forget me.

It moves like an artificial drone,
abundant punishment for the worship of noise.
Where is this music of the spheres?
Where are the dancers to reach and
 make a rise of these dry bones to song?

Remember the Flesh-pots of Egypt

Rubbing wrinkles
in an oiled spa
does not erase the marks.

The skin remembers slipping on the pyramids,
lifting, brick by block, one day after another,
fraying the arms, and numbering time into the creasing folds.

Freedom does not undo the harm
of old time sin, and the rise of new icons
golden with dangling mirrors foreseeing fate.

Repair could be on the way
fresh from the fleshpots of rescue;
Meanwhile, we eat our fill, steak by chop,
our minds still enslaved with memory.

145 Tofrinals

A moment of decease:
then the wild walk yearning
   for the other side of light

beyond the Public Land,
a race to the other side of
"No trespassing!"

Resting like a tragedy from Shakespeare
on an open ground of green moss, she thought:
so soft this bed, so tempting,
like the inner satin of a casket.

Laid out like a crucifix, the self-appointed martyr
of the rebel psyche, she sang a drugged chant:
Take me, take me,
take me to my home in the clouds.

A caught breath, and a cough
thundered realization into a retch:
I could die!

She began the long crawl back
to the blue kingdom of her couch,
and sleep.

Part Three

The Waiting Room

I

Leaning on the admissions desk, a bent elder
holds his arm inside his shirt covering his bandaged chest.
He squints at the bin of X-ray films,
winces at his coma-groans,
and shuffles past a gurney towards a curtained cubicle.

He blankets my husband, shivering from worry,
with empathy, and asks for the nurse.

Once at a funeral (not yet mine)
my mate reserved his chair with his hat,
folding it against a lowering life,
and rose to comfort a mourner.
In this cavernous room, tonight I am that empty chair.

Down the hall, an infant cries from the Oncology Unit.
His mother croons a soothing voice,
as the doctors work to repair the damage.

II

Code blue strikes
through the transparent double glass doors
mocking the need for privacy.
The nurse opens the stainless steel rim
reflecting a glisten of the fractured sky in its frame.

The slamming sound, like a fire alarm,
breaks into my head, calls for help, and stops.
I welcome the hollow silence
with a heart skip
and a steady beat.

III

A fast click of heels introduces the Chief,
the head honcho, the only man
in an impeccable tailored suit.
His white-coated aides hold and stack
the records neatly inside his leather brief case.

His bustle comes into focus;
the hallways clear a corridor
for his brisk walk and cheerful
"Good Morning, Good morning!"
He showers me with too much hope.

IV

I imagine Hari Krishnas chanting and close my eyes:
I greet a short dark man in street clothes,
made of squares, Legos to be exact,
who ministers to my veins as I float up,
dying to live among the clouds.

With my delirious flight,
I expand into a reveling blue.
In adoration, I spread out my spirit,
and I sink lazily into a soft silk sky,
until a steadfast booming voice disagrees:

"Return! You have a lot of work to do."
Obediently, I travel down
to find a body limp,
but swimming in hallucinations.

The Double Room

She shared a double with a lesbian,
who posed as a nymphomaniac,
and recited bedtime tales
about salacious exploits on her knees.

Down the hall, a dyke-like gal,
remembers herself
with no underpants straddling
her high school teachers.

The thirty-something cop,
the wife abuser,
notices that a young man
has the hots for her.

None of this is in her "treatment plan."
A mind takes at least three months to turn,
to even find the corner to turn.
Once having turned, it can begin its task.

She made six tiled boxes, with more to come.
She attended every group session.
She even ate take out pizza, planted a garden,
and hid safely from the New Age missionaries.

One morning, when the others were in church,
She tried to say the watchword prayer:
"Hear of Israel. God is One," but
a ratcheting wheel of sobs turned her mouth closed.

They imprisoned her mouth for one complete day.
Tomorrow, time will begin
with calls to the boarding houses
and visits to the halfway places.

My First Shrink Said ...

My first shrink said:
"Go scrub an encrusted pan!"
Sending him back behind his desk,
I rebuffed his pass and read him poetry.

Interviewing others to replace him,
I hired a woman behind a similar desk.
It was the décor that lured me,
or the same decorator.

Punishing me for tardiness one day,
she opened her door slowly and declared:
Insurance can't be billed for late appointments.
So I came later and later

until the charges mounted and I never paid.
Besting her, my mother-in-law.
frail from her heart's congestion,
called me, asked me for help.

Her daughter, immobile with shock,
waiting for her husband to die,
needed a mother, but her mother
was too sick.

Rising from my own cave,
I listed the food, both molding and fresh,
in her refrigerator, and made my nephews
laugh through their mourning.

Cheerful on his own deathbed,
my brother-in-law had willed:
"Let them take care of you."
Decades later my first shrink lost his license.

Her First Full-time Job

A single burner, a dorm room fridge,
and her first job – independence in a boarding house:
no more Passover Seders in a nut house;
no more group sessions with the shrink;

no more lesbian propositions in the night;
no more 24/7 coverage;
no more late night tears and confessions;
and no more withholding the real secrets

of warding off old seducing therapists
and fears of West coast orgies, encounter groups
and vacation rapes at Big Sur.

Relapse

The former escort worker,
the blond one with the perfect boobs,
and the abs-built body,
has seduced our attending psychiatrist.
In group, she decrees a patient ready

for a daily unattended outing:
fifteen minutes to walk toward the teen unit.
The fashionable E.R. nurse,
the one with the new cruise wardrobe,
demanding a spa treatment

for her cold-turkey drugless weekend,
hasn't a clue. But the teacher, the single mother,
the one with the fifteen-minute suicide watch,
sees, and begins to lie, like everyone else.
She needs to open her classroom on Monday,

and succumbs to the insurance rule
of the short term stay.
The staff, brimming with DSM paradigms,
declares the problem:
"She's been in therapy before!"

Group Therapy

My peers, the comforters come,
singly or in groups, arms outstretched,
eager to hug, to pacify,
to tell their own tales of suffering,
of sickness, and sometimes, of loss.

Some have ears that listen;
some even make a couch of silence.
Not many. Mostly their eyes covet sadness,
holding its fear over me like a dark halo
casting night around my brow.

I enter this room, receipt in hand,
all paid up for healing
to play with hope
and the comforting shelter
of wings to inspire me once again.

I Ask the Sky For Words

I ask the sky for words, and
the quality of dew falling on parched recall.

Once, as a teen babysitter,
my childhood molester appeared
when a child's touch
sent shivers through my groin.

My tongue locked in shock.
My hands froze, and I waited for reprieve.

Just yesterday, I saw a young boy,
training for the future in the greengrocer,
patting his father's crotch,
waiting for it to sprout.

Dad smiled down, called him naughty,
and chided him to stop.

Old memories, new memories release
into hidden metaphors,
which is all I can have.
They leap out from the night.

I wish for the inarticulate sound of snow
falling on a warm earth.

Frederick ("Fritz") Perls 1894-1970
The Father of Gestalt Therapy in America

Alas, old father figure of mine,
I remember you well at your final teaching
sick to your stomach, puking at dawn,
and again at lunch after the morning session.

You munched on salami in the kitchen with me,
ten months pregnant and offering tea.
No chicken soup for you, even near death.

Your followers worshiped you, the false idol,
and cheered your steely resistance to be healed.

You were cremated (how Buddhist!)
Ashes thrown to some cynical familial wind,
you left them nothing, no stone, no shrine,
only the ritual of projections, and possibilities.

Suffering a sea change, you loved the Esalen sulfur baths,
smelling for life, exploring young breasts.
Challenging you when you charged at me, The Village Idiot,
I cringed and folded like a soft toy.

In the Shadow of the Palm tree
For the Prophet Deborah

These fronds,
protective of the sun,
are no shield for conscience.

A warrior housewife,
wanting mercy,
I was brutal in my domain.

Luxuriant in the cool, the breeze sings
in a different key:
Could there have been another way?

Heaven must be a Stand of Lilies

Heaven must be a tall stand of rube-rum lilies,
their pink trumpets lifting fragrance
above the shoulders of my words.
Here, in this sanctuary, and now,
I sit hunched holding my conscience in my heart.

There are no lilies blooming on this carpet floor.

My memories strangle back my blood.
Another year may come, may even bring relief,
but not by this black belief, binding me with coma-sleep.
The white choice of sunlit skies is cast in frozen tears.

If I can see the lilies, I will live.

I afflict my soul and read the ritual list
of all I did, almost did, or didn't even do.
Like the first spade of dirt knocking on the coffin,
I hear a sound murmuring like a silent prayer.

I hope to hear the lilies turn to me.

I long for language to lift me like a shofar's blast,
to lift and alight me in a wisp of wind
that catches fragrance, pleases, and transforms,
like sacrifice into a perfume for the Force of all that lives.

The High Holy Day

You've set the sun too soon tonight.
My pockets still are full.
I still hold a silver purse
whose latch is tightly closed upon itself.

There's no time left, no time to covet
this one's dress, or that one's love,
no time to dust an evil tongue or two, abuse a child,
dishonor a parent or make a little more money.

The tarnish grows around this silver purse.

There are those who this past week fought for their lives:
Right now a doctor mends an open heart;
right here some soldier's arm is crooked against
a broken rib, his squadron fallen prey to terror.

But by my own hand I still live
and hold this graven clutch of grey,
a purse my father gave my mother, sixty years ago in love.

This piece of metal secretes some scraps of Yiddish
I can't read, engraved endearments to my mother,
my father's youthful photo, and a pocked mirror full of age.

In the glass, I watch me speechless walk the tightrope
between my conscience and my guilt.
I seek another image, unfolding, unlocking lights and suns,
from some mysterious source, something more than me.
some other self above myself, some turning to hold me safe
like a tallis at my grave.

The Pleading Time

This is the pleading time,
The show-of-conscience time,
The bleeding time of guilt,
The reminding remembering time,
The collecting-interest time,
The we-kept-our-promise time.

We beg.
We beseech.
We brag and strut our deeds;
We cancel all checks to plead our cause.

I remember a beggar, with an uncircumcised tongue
Stuttering anger with his staff, and screaming for water.
His sister whispered and sang to the rock who answered her
with the cool mercy of a gushing spring.

I remember our mothers and our fathers,
roaming the sandscape, parched with freedom
and bound to the rousing of the pillar and the fire.
They suspend their promises, and
annul all vows for the favor of womb-time grace and home.

Caught in a Cave

Caught in a sharpened man-made cave,
I dream of small sparks
chasing smoke from the unthawed light.

Cross-legged and open-palmed,
I close my eyes, redundant in a double dark.
My breath moves me like a lifeline out of guilt.

I breathe again and image a prayer shawl
floating down and fringing my back.
Knotted strings circle and lift my chest.

A glimpse of light cuts out a figure walking far ahead.
Is this my guide Elijah in disguise and dressed like me?
Visions propel me forward, calling for help,

but only echoes answer as my flight takes hold.
I don't remember standing up;
I don't remember being bruised.

I think I see a bright and shining mist.
Is this a mirror or a doorway to the sky?
I edge out, slowing to a crawl; I sprawl only inches from the ledge.

Below is valley; above are fiery letters piercing stone.
The sky rolls out its sun, redeeming me.
I start to climb the never-ending path.

The Yellow Thread

"a yellow thread, as authoritative
as God is supposed to be ..."
"Rain," by Mary Oliver

Shedding the scales of disappointment and betrayal,
I inch towards the kitchen to make his favorite soup.

An overfilled box of carrots pulls me along,
and the onions are so good for tears.
I love my damp wet face watching
these split dried old peas roil
and melt into a sunrise of moving rust.

And yes, the crushing of the cloves,
taming the sharp raw garlic
with an undulating wake of bubbles.
The long simmer uncovers
the deep sweet root of parsnips.

I forgot the quick sneak of bouillon.
Please don't tell him!

Now, with my broth simmering,
I can hear again and wait
for words to green the walls with sound.

Part Four

Before the Crossing

There is a song resting and rocking the warm air
that I hear but can't quite sing.
It enters me from out of old volcanic rock
as dense as the dark past;

I've felt it in Hebraic cantillations,
in the rising and the falling
of a scribe writing on parchment; I know it
like my own blood running unseen
in the hidden chambers of my ribs;

Could it resound like thunder, appear as fire,
become a pillar, a cloud, or even death?
The bible says choose life, walk between
the parting waves, move like a minstrel
to the music that I am, have been,

and always will be.

The Sitting Bones

I

I have planted my sitting bones equally on the chair;
a bench challenges my knees, confronting flexibility.
It's my favorite chair, with my favorite pillow
softly on the floor.
Both feet position and uncross.

My palms are resting in an open mudra, and
my belly has too much spirit; I flatten it
against my spine.
This is harder than it looks.

Relax, says the guru. I respond with doubt.
Inhale and pause, he says; *exhale and pause*.

I hyperventilate
and hold my breath. I wish for torpor;
to the statue before me, this is a deadly sin.

Old thoughts in new paradigms become a refuge of despair.
Each breath unclothes another; each layer advertises revelation.
Neurosis is a bad habit, an obstacle to watch like a movie
with a willing suspension of disbelief.

My new therapy becomes
a thin membrane of hope,
dreaming possibilities.

II

Affirmations: I must envision my best moment, my best love,
the birth of my best new love,
my children's expansive smiles,
a plant budded from a seed,
a landscape newly colored by the dawn,
or a sunset carrying rebirth, -
any new arising will do.

III

The instruction manual for
the rocky road to enlightenment
did not explain to the starry eyed devotees,
the torture on the way:

the long history of furnaces shedding dust
the dark night of recovered flashbacks,
the heartbreak opening in the chambers of loss,
or the wordless awe of terror.

Where is the winged oracle when you need her?
Where is this undoing into an open space?

I can only edge towards patience through the fog;
with the slow breathing of my sangha
I try to make a friend of fear.

IV

I am lighting incense in my son's old bedroom.
The Buddha, less an idol than a reminder,
looks down on my slow attempts to build a new belief.

I know before whom I sit, and before whom I supplicate.

I see an altar with the horns of Law rising.
I approach at my own risk.

I Miss the Dreams
For my mother

I miss the dreams you meant to me;
the hope of future times
will never roll from me again at night.
I'll never say
that the bright and cloudless sky
will soon see you –
a younger, better you.

What's really gone is bones and flesh –
and warmth. I can't remember warmth;
I only have this cool and chilly shock:
   a blank absence,
   a closeness to the void
   that I don't want, and then
   the drum call of earth on wood.

I walk by water, and the waves have wet my feet.
My prints are smoothed away behind me.
Soon I search again for that underside of memory.

A Letter to Mark Reich*

I killed the Calla Lilies you gave me.
I warned you they were beyond my care.
I couldn't break into the heart of the soil in the fall,
I couldn't separate the mats around its drying root
still holding life with a full head of threads.

I had no cool place to house it for a whole winter.
I had no faith that birth was dormant in a drying seed.

Unlike Katherine Hepburn in that old film, I can't ever say:
"The Callas Lilies are in bloom again!"**

I'm sorry. I was no comfort to a fellow gardener.

But those scrawny yellow Angel Hairs thrived!
Without my care, those variegated seedlings
shaded and colored to any sense of sunlight,
held fast to the light and even to the dark of it.

They slowly reached out to every fertile hidden speck of earth,
holding each shimmer of wind,
moving with will toward the edge of my life,
hugging the tall Rhododendron stalks secretly at the root;
They loved the shady Viburnum.

Those spiked stars could crawl, touch, root,
and cover the whole shady ground beneath.
Mark, see how the wings fold in and out to climb my house.
They warm it, lingering long and soft,
like my memories of you.

* Mark Reich, at 50, succumbed to MS after a lifetime of fighting it.
** "Stage Door" 1937

Lilith Rising

I

Writing another letter to Adam,
I remind him how warmly I seeded his solitude,
Crooning into his ear, and sung him sweet songs.
After all, I *was* his first love, and his *match*.
Even if it was an arranged marriage,
even though the angels threw me out,
the apples never tempted me.

Slithering and suggesting new words,
the snake hit on me first, but I knew right from wrong.
Adam, you were a fickle reed, listening to every wind she blew.

Equal was not your thing; you loved that
chauvinist master-slave game.
I miss the garden more than you.
The more I spoke my mind,
the more you stroked your rib,
and your navel too.

II

I called Yah on you,
but that unleashed a wind that flew me away
to the Sea of Reeds, until you missed me, your shrew,
and called me back. Three angels pleaded for my return.
With chastening severity, they told me to subdue my voice,
my mind, and my democratic ways; they threatened me
with a new chance, and slew all my newly birthed children,
my colony of souls; they called them devil boys.

I no longer prowl in mirrors for Eve's new seed.
Not really cruel at heart, I promised kindness
before the kidnap.
Now I serve a new master
who feeds me and my kin, who promises light,
a codependent arising of redemption, an easier life of Dharma.

Walking sleepless in my dreams of you,
I still circle each month, alone, apart, before I weep.

My Vine-ripened Mother

I

This tomato is for you,
this luck of beefy fruit,
scalloped over eggs
that frames a remembrance:

The market full of harvest
and you, cruising for a bargain.
You talked the farmer,
soil beneath his nails,
from his brimful basket
full of warmth,
fresh from a late picking.

Next breakfast my sleepover friend
had never seen these rosy plums
inappropriate abundance, with toast.
I shamed for your old-world ways,
spilling over saucers for a guest.

I cannot eat too much of these,
the blush-red and vine-ripened memories of you;
I relish them for breakfast, lunch,
and night-time snack.

You were the pick-of-the-crop;
your heritage has left me stout
with richness.

II

These are not my hands,
these cracked and creviced claws;
they have no wrists, just
padded tunnels, carping at each turn.

I can barely lift them
to the new blooms of spring,
who yes to you and no to me.
I drag them towards my shrunken frame.

59

Just when did I get these
stunted limbs with their failing force?
Just when? Was it at your grave
when my thud of soil cut off our bond?

Or was it when you could no longer walk,
shocked into a wheeling chair?
Or maybe at the howling day of my birth,
when you clutched the pillar posted with my name?

These are your hands!
You always made a show of them to me,
when, after a hard work, they ached,
pulsed against your skin, and cracked with age.

And now I remember you praising purple,
cutting back the lilac trees,
pruning off their flowerlets.

For I remember how you fondled spring,
smelling these purple hearts
saying goodbye to every leaf and tree,
and even to the sky that domed my yard,
when I, with two full fives full,
gave you armloads of soon-to-be yellow forsythia.

May Pardes* be your garden now,
planting and pruning in the always new,
and ever-abundant growth.

* Pardes is the Hebrew name for the Garden of Eden, where, according to legend,
some souls live after the death of their bodies.

III

As long as comfort lives
And cruelty lies,
You did not really die.

A gesture makes reborn
your hands. A sight,
a look, and I know
you did not really die.

You return to me
in my children's tears,
and in my voice, you sigh.

Daily, when I hold your silvered glass,
I see my heritage is in my hair,
like yours, it will never grey;
I have a halo crowned by you.

I swear by memories past,
and love that lasts beyond repair,
as long as words survive,
and shofars sound of souls reborn,
you, who gave me life,
will never really die.

Let Me Not Be Afraid
A Prayer to Pray

Let me not be afraid of Your letters,
All fire, all brimstone;
Without parchment, without bone,
They are as fleshless, as I am alone.

They breathe, and I hear that formless echo
Sparking images of the first creation.
They move, and all sensation
Becomes a silent rush toward the curved embrace of time.

If I could close my eyes and remember You
Who can light a bush and not consume,
Who with your fingers can make the tablets bloom
With holiness, I could draw warmth from a stone,

Or better yet, a rock; I could get honey from
A rock; I could wrestle with an angel,
Know my true name and not fall
A victim to this wall of chatter.

                          An easy prayer
Would be a bridge to You, my source, my love.
Help me curl my mouth around that seed.
I've lost my youth in search of inspiration.

Give me the power of the first aleph,
The soundless sound before the first word,
The first word that was wind, and the first silence
Before my long journey into meaning.

Sunday August 6, 2006
Beyond our Refuge: Vipassyana Retreat at the Insight Meditation Center

I

The ground bears and buoys an ocean of shaded ferns,
waving at each whim of the wind,
allowing a spruced-up armada of pines,
with branches spiked amid the intermittent clouds.
They sail along on an endless blue beyond my reach.
Decked out on my giant rock,
I ride the forest, believing I am in command.

II

A devotee, motley in saffron and maroon,
pillow in his armpit, bandana wrapping his shaved skull,
fins through the needled course eyeing the goal behind me:
lighter minds work the clanking kitchen,
in the blond boards of the meditation hall,
and especially in cleaning toilets.

III

Cynically, walking slowly like a snail, I resume my practice.
A striped chipmunk, full of the moment, trembles to a stop,
alerts his still claws at his chest and waits on his haunches.
Are those five long-nailed fingers?
Is that a thumb twitching for alms?
With no bowl to allay the hunger, I am empty;
I turn to him for refuge.

April 20, 2007
In the Meditation Hall: At Bhante Gunaratana's Silent 10-day Jhana Retreat

Mother, Father, are you here?
Sister, Brother, have you come too?
Have you brought our Holocaust family,
long gone from their charred bodies?

Bhante G calls in the all the *Devas*,
and the Bodhisattvas too.
He loves their Pali names.

I am afraid of the Buddha;
I call on all of you for help
against a mere chill from an open window.

Even the mystical rabbis
whom I've studied for decades,
are without their wordplay
in this sangha of silence Without End. *

But who have my fellow congregants called in?
The room is crowded with quiet tears,
and mine erupt into the noiseless walk of counted breaths.

Hear O Israel.

You can hear the unshackling
of the fettered shells * of the mind.

---

* "Without End" is the translation for the mystical Jewish name of God: "Ayn Sof."
* "Shells" is the translation for "Klepot," the shells that imprison the spirit.

Shambhala in the Sky with Diamonds: Buddha in a Tallis

I dream of Dharamsala and the Temple rebuilt,
the Himalayas born from a single *Ohm*,
and Shambhala sparkling in its foothills.

Floating above is Elijah's six-winged wheeled chariot
over the ashes of Falloujah,
once the Aramaic Yeshiva town of Pumbedita,*
the Babylonian mouth of learning,
on the bank of the River Euphrates,
(a mere 40 miles from the Tigris)
sits Buddha in a Tallis.

In Archangel Metatron's throne
his mantra is – Amen.

*After the destruction of the second temple in Jerusalem, Pumbedita was the
  Important center of Jewish learning from the third century to the ninth
  century

Build My Spine

She walks with me
as we crumble dried leaves together.
They form seed-blankets on the roots of trees.

I hear the snap of falling life;
I image a bright shimmering in a sky
bowered by roses.

To breath again without awe,
to let the breath breathe me
before the tongue can speak,
is a silent gift from the queen of mercy
returning me to myself.

Language is a ladder,
colored rung by fragrant step, -
strings of clear light, -
that builds my spine.

A Symphony of Words

Before the tongue can speak,
I wait for the silent gift:

Language is a ladder,
Colored rung by fragrant step,

Strings of clear light
Build my spine and

Serenade me home.